2023 by T.L. Ellibourck. All rights reserved

Paige and squinty is a fun children's book covering adventure, history and cooking basic recipes for parents and children to bond together.

No part of this book shall be used for photocopying or recordings without written permission from the author, except for inclusion of brief quotations in a review.

For permissions requests write to the author, address below:

Natasha Elliott
Flat 3 37 cheriton road
Folkestone Kent CT201DD
First published July 2023
Printed in the United Kingdom

Dedication Page:

This book is dedicated to my partner who has always believed in me.

RECIPE

For Poolish
200g strong white bread flour
1/2 tsp easy bake yeast from 7g sachet

For Baguettes
200g plain white flour
250g strong white flour, plus extra for dusting and folding
the rest of the yeast from 7g sachet
1 1/2 tsp fine salt
More flour for dusting

METHOD

STEP 1
to make poolish, mix the flour and yeast in a bowl. Add 200ml room temperature water and stir to a very thick batter. Cover with cling film then chill overnight, after which the batter will have doubled in size.

STEP 2
The next day, combine the flours remaining yeast and the salt in to a bowl. Add another 25oml water to the poolish, then pour into the flours mix to make very wet, sloppy dough. Let this sit for 20mins, which helps the dough come together more quickly when you fold.

STEP 3
After 20mins the dough will still be wet this is good for a good baguette. Fold for 10mins, or use a mixer with a dough hook for 5-8mins, until dough is firm but smooth and elastic.

STEP 4
Dust a clean side with flour and the dough then fold the dough inwards to make a ball. Transfer to a lightly floured bowl and cover with a clean teatowel and let rise for 1 1/2 hours until double in size.

STEP 5
Dust a heavy teatowel or bakers cloth with lots of flour, and put it onto a large kitchen tray. Shape three longe, baguette-width ridges in cloth. Turn the dough onto the floured worktop then flour the sticky side. Cut into 3 equal pieces using large knife. Do Not Knead The Dough!

STEP 6
Working on one at a time, press each piece into an oval 25cm long and 20cm deep. Fold one side into the middle and press down well. Fold other same way, make a long strip of dough with a groove down the centre. Now fold over itself length ways like a sausage, pressing two sides together well in a tight seam against the worktop. Roll lightly under palm to seal and make ends pointy. Should be about 40cm long.

STEP 7
Place dough seam side down in your prepared cloth, then repeat. Dust all baguettes with flour, cover and leave for 1 hour until doubled in size.

STEP 8
Heat oven 240C gas 9. Put a roasting tin on the shelf towards the bottom, plus set a shelf in the top third. Scatter flour over a baking tray. Carefully roll or lift the baguettes into the trays.

STEP 9
With a knife slash baguettes diagonally 5-6 times. Add 100ml water to the baking tray and close door quickly and bake for 20mins or until dark, golden and crispy. Once ready place on cooling rack and enjoy same day.

Recipe is taken from BBC good food and not my recipe

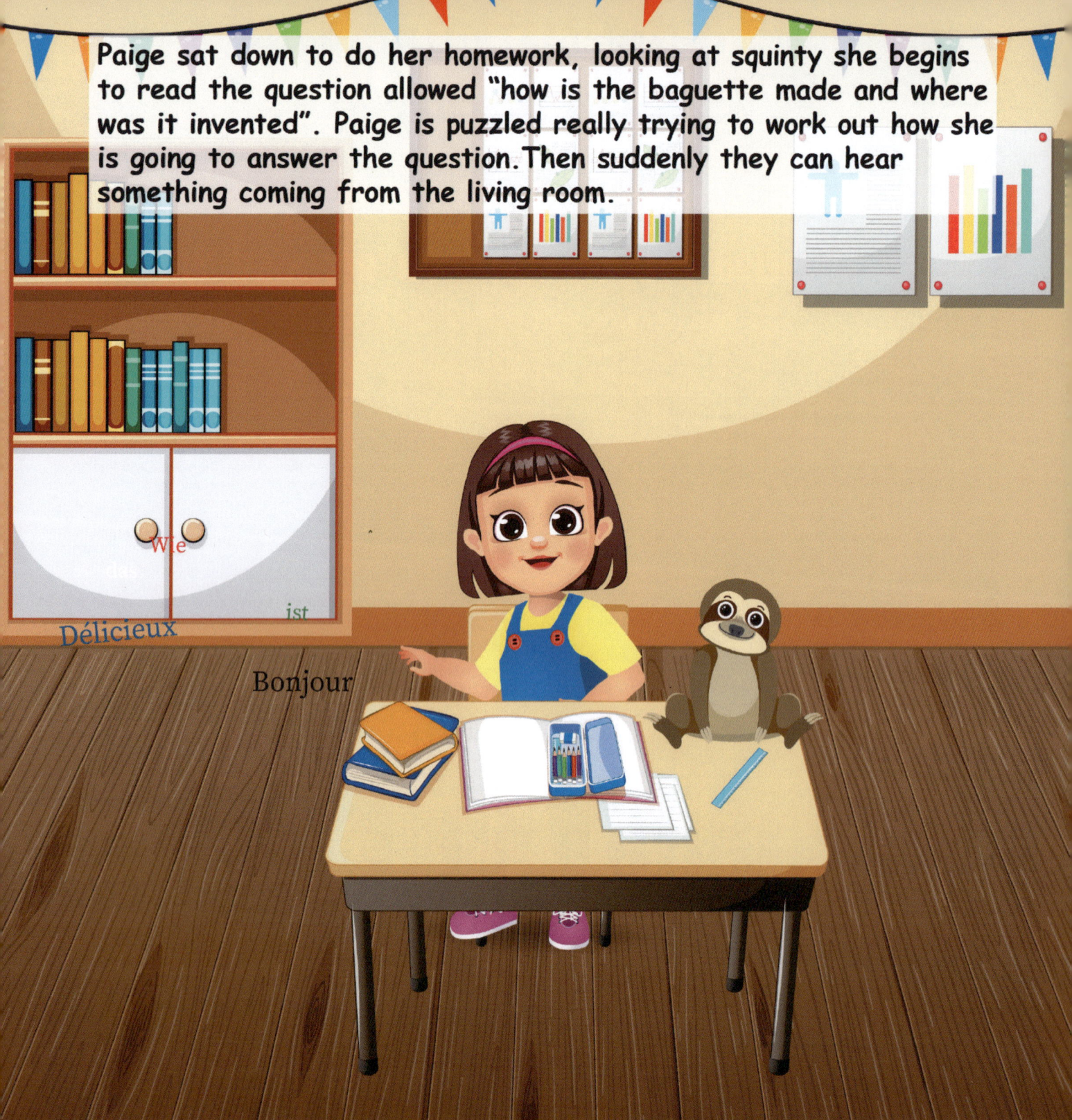

Paige sat down to do her homework, looking at squinty she begins to read the question allowed "how is the baguette made and where was it invented". Paige is puzzled really trying to work out how she is going to answer the question. Then suddenly they can hear something coming from the living room.

Wind gushes in and the room begins to spin they are spiralling out of control. Things are flying passed so fast it's hard to see what is happening.

Paige and squinty finally stop spinning and they find themselves in front of the Eiffel Tower in Paris, France. "How did we end up here squinty". Squinty just shrugs and looks confused.

"Bonjour" that's French for hello.
" My name is Napoleon Bonaparte, I invented the baguette in 1920". Napoleon created the shape for soldiers during the war to make it easy to carry. "Would you like to learn more" Napoleon asks. Paige and Squinty nod their heads.

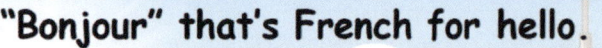

Napoleon had waved his baguette and they all found themselves in a kitchen. "Did you know that French law states you must only use four ingredients to make baguettes and they must be 65cm in length, also there is no baking between 10pm and 4am".

Paige and Squinty look very puzzled. "Are we going to make baguettes Squinty". "I hope so, that would be really cool". Napoleon gives them the recipe and Paige and Squinty now must learn how to make the baguettes. "Would you like to learn with us?. Just follow the recipe on page 5". Paige has mixed the ingredients and Squinty folds the dough. They then place them in the oven..

The baguettes are now in the oven and Paige and squinty must clean up the kitchen. " Wow that was fun squinty, we actually made our own baguettes".

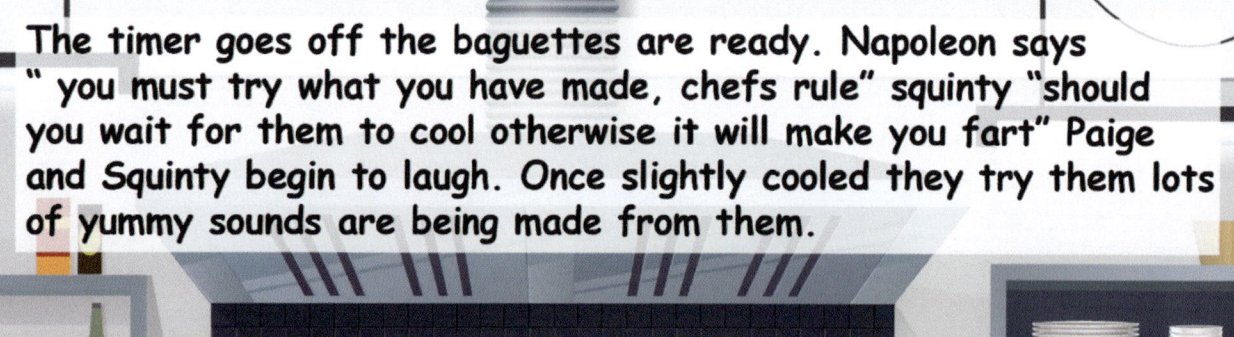

The timer goes off the baguettes are ready. Napoleon says " you must try what you have made, chefs rule" squinty "should you wait for them to cool otherwise it will make you fart" Paige and Squinty begin to laugh. Once slightly cooled they try them lots of yummy sounds are being made from them.

Napoleon had waved the baguette again and they found themselves outside a Boulangerie a shop that sells the baguettes.
"This is where they go to be sold". " This is so cool squinty we get to go into a shop and see our baguettes being sold".

Inside the shop Paige and Squinty browse and look to buy some fromage and jambon, cheese and ham to go with their baguettes. "I must say au revoir that's goodbye". Then Napoleon vanished as fast as he appeared.

Paige and Squinty start having a sword fight with the baguettes. "Take that" wack, pow "I win" says Squinty. They decide to lay down on the grass and close their eyes for a moment.

They wake and they are back in the classroom where they began.

" What just happened did I dream that or did we really go to France and make baguettes" " I dreamt it too" says Squinty. " We cannot have both had the same dream, wow". Shocked and happy Paige now knows what to write for her home work.

Next time come with us to Italy to learn how to make Pizza

Printed in Great Britain
by Amazon